Ein
Gebetbuch

A Simple Prayer Book

ENGLISH - DEUTSCH

*All booklets are published thanks to the
generous support of the members of the
Catholic Truth Society*

CATHOLIC TRUTH SOCIETY
PUBLISHERS TO THE HOLY SEE

Contents

Inhalt

BASIC PRAYERS

Our Father

Our Father, who art in heaven, hallowed be thy name. Thy Kingdom come. Thy will be done on earth as it is in heaven. Give us this day our daily bread, and forgive us our trespasses, as we forgive those who trespass against us, and lead us not into temptation, but deliver us from evil. Amen.

Hail Mary

Hail, Mary, full of grace, the Lord is with thee: blessed art thou among women, and blessed is the fruit of thy womb, Jesus. Holy Mary, Mother of God, pray for us sinners, now, and at the hour of our death. Amen.

Glory be to the Father

Glory be to the Father, and to the Son, and to the Holy Spirit. As it was in the beginning, is now, and ever shall be, world without end. Amen.

GRUNDGEBETE

Vater unser

Vater unser im Himmel, geheiligt werde dein Name, dein Reich komme, dein Wille geschehe wie im Himmel, so auch auf Erden. Unser tägliches Brot gib uns heute und vergib uns unsere Schuld, wie auch wir vergeben unseren Schuldigern. Und führe uns nicht in Versuchung, sondern erlöse uns von dem Bösen. Amen.

Gegrüßet seist du, Maria

Gegrüßet seist du, Maria, voll der Gnade, der Herr ist mit dir, du bist gebenedeit unter den Frauen, und gebenedeit ist die Frucht deines Leibes, Jesus. Heilige Maria, Mutter Gottes, bitte für uns Sünder jetzt und in der Stunde unseres Todes. Amen.

Ehre sei dem Vater

Ehre sei dem Vater und dem Sohne und dem Heiligen Geist, wie es war im Anfang, so auch jetzt und alle Zeit und in Ewigkeit. Amen.

THE ORDER OF MASS

INTRODUCTORY RITES

The faithful dispose themselves properly to celebrate the Eucharist.

Before Mass begins, the people gather in a spirit of recollection, preparing for their participation in the Mass. All stand during the entrance procession.

Sign of the Cross

After the Entrance Chant, the Priest and the faithful sign themselves with the Sign of the Cross:

Priest: In the name of the Father, and of the Son, and of the Holy Spirit.

Response: Amen.

Greeting

The Priest greets the people, with one of the following:

1. Pr. The grace of our Lord Jesus Christ,
and the love of God,
and the communion of the Holy Spirit
be with you all.

2. Pr. Grace to you and peace from God our Father
and the Lord Jesus Christ.

3. Pr. The Lord be with you.

The people reply:

R. And with your spirit.

— DER ABLAUF DES GOTTESDIENSTES —

ERÖFFNUNG

Zum Einzug stehen die Gläubigen auf und singen einen Hymnus.

Priester: Im Namen des Vaters und des Sohnes und des Heiligen Geistes.
Antwort: Amen.

Pr: Die Gnade unseres Herrn Jesus Christus, die Liebe Gottes, des Vaters, und die Gemeinschaft des Heiligen Geistes sei mit euch.
A: Und mit deinem Geiste.

The Priest, or a Deacon, or another minister, may very briefly introduce the faithful to the Mass of the day.

Penitential Act

There are three forms of the Penitential Act which may be chosen from as appropriate.

Pr. Brethren (brothers and sisters),
    let us acknowledge our sins,
and so prepare ourselves to celebrate the sacred mysteries.
A brief pause for silence follows.
Then one of the following forms is used:

---

1. I confess to almighty God
and to you, my brothers and sisters,
that I have greatly sinned,
in my thoughts and in my words,
in what I have done and in what I have failed to do,
(*and, striking their breast, they say*:)
through my fault, through my fault,
through my most grievous fault;
therefore I ask blessed Mary ever-Virgin,
all the Angels and Saints,
and you, my brothers and sisters,
to pray for me to the Lord our God.

---

2. Pr. Have mercy on us, O Lord.
R. For we have sinned against you.
Pr. Show us, O Lord, your mercy.
R. And grant us your salvation.

Allgemeines Schuldbekenntnis

Pr: Brüder und Schwestern, damit wir die heiligen Geheimnisse in rechter Weise feiern können, wollen wir bekennen, dass wir gesündigt haben.

Ich bekenne Gott, dem Allmächtigen,
und allen Brüdern und Schwestern,
dass ich Gutes unterlassen und Böses getan habe.
Ich habe gesündigt in Gedanken,
Worten und Werken durch meine Schuld,
durch meine Schuld,
durch meine große Schuld.
Darum bitte ich die selige Jungfrau Maria,
alle Engel und Heiligen und euch,
Brüder und Schwestern,
für mich zu beten bei Gott,
unserem Herrn.

Pr: Der Herr erbarme sich unser,
er nehme von uns Sünde und Schuld,
damit wir mit reinem Herzen diese Feier begehen.
A: Amen.

Invocations naming the gracious works of the Lord may be made, as in the example below:

3. Pr. You were sent to heal the contrite of heart:

Lord, have mercy.   *Or:*   Kyrie, eleison.

R. Lord, have mercy.   *Or:*   **Kyrie, eleison.**

Pr. You came to call sinners:

Christ, have mercy.   *Or:*   Christe, eleison.

R. Christ, have mercy.   *Or:*   **Christe, eleison.**

Pr. You are seated at the right hand of the Father to intercede for us:

Lord, have mercy.   *Or:*   Kyrie, eleison.

R. Lord, have mercy.   *Or:*   **Kyrie, eleison.**

The absolution by the Priest follows:

Pr. May almighty God have mercy on us,

forgive us our sins,

and bring us to everlasting life.

R. Amen.

The Kyrie, eleison *(*Lord, have mercy*) invocations follow, unless they have just occurred.*

Pr. Lord, have mercy.   **R. Lord, have mercy.**

Pr. Christ, have mercy.   **R. Christ, have mercy.**

Pr. Lord, have mercy.   **R. Lord, have mercy.**

Or:

Pr. Kyrie, eleison.   **R. Kyrie, eleison.**

Pr. Christe, eleison.   **R. Christe, eleison.**

Pr. Kyrie, eleison.   **R. Kyrie, eleison.**

Es folgen die Kyrie-Rufe
Pr: Herr, erbarme dich (unser).
A: Herr, erbarme dich (unser).
Pr: Christus, erbarme dich (unser).
A: Christus, erbarme dich (unser).
Pr: Herr, erbarme dich (unser).
A: Herr, erbarme dich (unser).

The Gloria

*On Sundays (outside of Advent and Lent), Solemnities and
Feast Days, this hymn is either sung or said:*

Glory to God in the highest,
and on earth peace to people of good will.

We praise you,
we bless you,
we adore you,
we glorify you,
we give you thanks for your great glory,
Lord God, heavenly King,
O God, almighty Father.

Lord Jesus Christ, Only Begotten Son,
Lord God, Lamb of God, Son of the Father,
you take away the sins of the world, have mercy on us;
you take away the sins of the world, receive our prayer;
you are seated at the right hand of the Father,
    have mercy on us.
For you alone are the Holy One,
you alone are the Lord,
you alone are the Most High,
Jesus Christ,
with the Holy Spirit,
in the glory of God the Father.
Amen.

Gloria

Das Gloria wird gesungen oder gebetet, wenn dies vorgesehen ist:

Ehre sei Gott in der Höhe und Friede auf Erden den Menschen seiner Gnade.

Wir loben dich, wir preisen dich,

wir beten dich an,

wir rühmen dich und danken dir,

denn groß ist deine Herrlichkeit:

Herr und Gott, König des Himmels,

Gott und Vater, Herrscher über das All,

Herr, eingeborener Sohn, Jesus Christus.

Herr und Gott, Lamm Gottes,

Sohn des Vaters,

du nimmst hinweg die Sünde der Welt:

erbarme dich unser,

du nimmst hinweg die Sünde der Welt:

nimm an unser Gebet,

du sitzest zur Rechten des Vaters:

erbarme dich unser.

Denn du allein bist der Heilige,

du allein der Herr,

du allein der Höchste:

Jesus Christus,

mit dem Heiligen Geist,

zur Ehre Gottes des Vaters. Amen.

When this hymn is concluded, the Priest, says:
Pr. Let us pray.
And all pray in silence. Then the Priest says the Collect prayer, which ends:
R. Amen.

THE LITURGY OF THE WORD

By hearing the word proclaimed in worship, the faithful again enter into a dialogue with God.

First Reading

The reader goes to the ambo and proclaims the First Reading, while all sit and listen. The reader ends:
The word of the Lord.
R. Thanks be to God.
It is appropriate to have a brief time of quiet between readings as those present take the word of God to heart.

Psalm

The psalmist or cantor sings or says the Psalm, with the people making the response.

Second Reading

On Sundays and certain other days there is a second reading. It concludes with the same response as above.

Gospel

The assembly stands for the Gospel Acclamation. Except during Lent the Acclamation is:
R. Alleluia

Der Priester spricht: Lasset uns beten.
Alle beten leise mit dem Priester. Dann spricht der Priester das Tagesgebet und beendet dies mit den Worten:
Pr: von Ewigkeit zu Ewigkeit.
A: Amen.

WORTGOTTESDIENST

Die Gläubigen setzen sich zur ersten Lesung. Am Ende der Lesung spricht der Lektor:

Lektor: Wort des lebendigen Gottes.
A: Dank sei Gott.
Dann folgt der Antwortpsalm. Die Gemeinde übernimmt den Kehrvers. Ist eine zweite Lesung vorgesehen, so endet diese wie die erste:

Lektor: Wort des lebendigen Gottes.
A: Dank sei Gott.

Nun folgt als zweiter Zwischengesang das Halleluja bzw. der an dessen Stelle vorgesehene andere Gesang. Die Gläubigen stehen.

During Lent the following forms are used:

R. Praise to you, O Christ, king of eternal glory! *Or*:

R. Praise and honour to you, Lord Jesus! *Or*:

R. Glory and praise to you, O Christ! *Or*:

R. Glory to you, O Christ, you are the Word of God!

At the ambo the Deacon, or the Priest says:

Pr. The Lord be with you.

R. And with your spirit.

Pr. A reading from the holy Gospel according to *N*.

He makes the Sign of the Cross on the book and, together with the people, on his forehead, lips, and breast.

R. Glory to you, O Lord.

At the end of the Gospel:

Pr. The Gospel of the Lord.

R. Praise to you, Lord Jesus Christ.

After the Gospel all sit to listen to the homily.

The Homily

Then follows the Homily, which is preached by a Priest or Deacon on all Sundays and Holydays of Obligation. After a brief silence all stand.

The Creed

On Sundays and Solemnities, the Profession of Faith will follow. The Apostles' Creed may be used.

Pr: Der Herr sei mit euch.
A: Und mit deinem Geiste.
Pr: Aus dem heiligen Evangelium nach *N.*
A: Ehre sei dir, o Herr.

Am Ende des Evangeliums:
Pr: Evangelium unseres Herrn Jesus Christus.
A: Lob sei dir, Christus.
An Sonn- und Feiertagen folgt eine Predigt.

Homilie

Credo

The Niceno-Constantinopolitan Creed

I believe in one God,
the Father almighty,
maker of heaven and earth,
of all things visible and invisible.

I believe in one Lord Jesus Christ,
the Only Begotten Son of God,
born of the Father before all ages.
God from God, Light from Light,
true God from true God,
begotten, not made, consubstantial with the Father;
through him all things were made.
For us men and for our salvation
he came down from heaven, (*all bow*)
and by the Holy Spirit was incarnate of the Virgin Mary,
and became man.

For our sake he was crucified under Pontius Pilate,
he suffered death and was buried,
and rose again on the third day
in accordance with the Scriptures.
He ascended into heaven
and is seated at the right hand of the Father.
He will come again in glory
to judge the living and the dead
and his kingdom will have no end.

I believe in the Holy Spirit, the Lord, the giver of life,
who proceeds from the Father and the Son,

Wir glauben an den einen Gott,
den Vater, den Allmächtigen,
der alles geschaffen hat, Himmel und Erde,
die sichtbare und die unsichtbare Welt.
Und an den einen Herrn Jesus Christus,
Gottes eingeborenen Sohn,
aus dem Vater geboren vor aller Zeit:
Gott von Gott, Licht vom Licht,
wahrer Gott vom wahren Gott, gezeugt,
nicht geschaffen, eines Wesens mit dem Vater;
durch ihn ist alles geschaffen.

Für uns Menschen und zu unserem Heil ist er vom
Himmel gekommen,
(Zu den folgenden Worten verbeugen sich alle)
hat Fleisch angenommen durch den Heiligen Geist von
der Jungfrau Maria und ist Mensch geworden.
Er wurde für uns gekreuzigt unter Pontius Pilatus,
hat gelitten und ist begraben worden,
ist am dritten Tage auferstanden nach der Schrift und
aufgefahren in den Himmel.
Er sitzt zur Rechten des Vaters und wird
wiederkommen in Herrlichkeit,
zu richten die Lebenden und die Toten;
seiner Herrschaft wird kein Ende sein.

Wir glauben an den Heiligen Geist,
der Herr ist und lebendig macht,
der aus dem Vater und dem Sohn hervorgeht,

who with the Father and the Son is adored and glorified,
who has spoken through the prophets.

I believe in one, holy, catholic and apostolic Church.
I confess one Baptism for the forgiveness of sins
and I look forward to the resurrection of the dead
and the life of the world to come. Amen.

The Apostles' Creed

I believe in God,
the Father almighty
Creator of heaven and earth,
and in Jesus Christ, his only Son, our Lord, (*all bow*)
who was conceived by the Holy Spirit,
born of the Virgin Mary,
suffered under Pontius Pilate,
was crucified, died and was buried;
he descended into hell;
on the third day he rose again from the dead;
he ascended into heaven,
and is seated at the right hand of God
    the Father almighty;
from there he will come to judge the living and the dead.

I believe in the Holy Spirit,
the holy catholic Church,
the communion of saints,
the forgiveness of sins,
the resurrection of the body,
and life everlasting. Amen.

der mit dem Vater und dem Sohn angebetet und
verherrlicht wird,
der gesprochen hat durch die Propheten,
und die eine, heilige, katholische und apostolische Kirche.
Wir bekennen die eine Taufe zur Vergebung der Sünden.
Wir erwarten die Auferstehung der Toten und das
Leben der kommenden Welt. Amen.

Das Apostolische Glaubensbekenntnis

Ich glaube an Gott, den Vater, den Allmächtigen, den
Schöpfer des Himmels und der Erde,
und an Jesus Christus, seinen eingeborenen Sohn,
unsern Herrn, empfangen durch den Heiligen Geist,
geboren von der Jungfrau Maria,
gelitten unter Pontius Pilatus,
gekreuzigt, gestorben und begraben,
hinabgestiegen in das Reich des Todes,
am dritten Tage auferstanden von den Toten,
aufgefahren in den Himmel.
Er sitzt zur Rechten Gottes,
des allmächtigen Vaters,
von dort wird er kommen,
zu richten die Lebenden und die Toten.

Ich glaube an den Heiligen Geist,
die heilige katholische Kirche,
Gemeinschaft der Heiligen, Vergebung der Sünden,
Auferstehung der Toten,
und das ewige Leben. Amen.

The Prayer of the Faithful (Bidding Prayers)

Intentions will normally be for the Church; for the world; for those in particular need; and for the local community. After each there is time for silent prayer, followed by the next intention, or concluded with a sung phrase such as **Christ, hear us***, or* **Christ graciously hear us***, or by a responsory such as:*

Let us pray to the Lord.

R. Grant this, almighty God. *Or:*

R. Lord, have mercy. *Or:*

R. Kyrie, eleison.

The Priest concludes the Prayer with a collect.

THE LITURGY OF THE EUCHARIST

For Catholics, the Eucharist is the source and summit of the whole Christian Life.

After the Liturgy of the Word, the people sit and the Offertory Chant begins. The faithful express their participation by making an offering, bringing forward bread and wine for the celebration of the Eucharist.

Preparatory Prayers

Standing at the altar, the Priest takes the paten with the bread and holds it slightly raised above the altar with both hands, saying:

Fürbitten

Die Fürbitten werden vorgetragen. Nach jeder Fürbitte folgt eine kurze Zeit des stillen Gebets, danach die Bitte:

V: Christus, höre uns. *oder:* **V:** Wir bitten Dich,
A: Christus, erhöre uns. *oder:* **A: erhöre uns.**

EUCHARISTIEFEIER

Gabenbereitung

Das Herbeibringen und die Bereitung der Gaben können von einer entsprechenden Antiphon zur Gabenbereitung (oder ein Hymnus) begleitet werden. Die Gläubigen sitzen. Wenn kein Gesang vorgesehen ist, kann der Priester die folgenden Gebete laut sprechen.

Pr. Blessed are you, Lord God of all creation,
for through your goodness we have received
the bread we offer you:
fruit of the earth and work of human hands,
it will become for us the bread of life.

R. Blessed be God for ever.

The Priest then takes the chalice and holds it slightly raised above the altar with both hands, saying:

Pr. Blessed are you, Lord God of all creation,
for through your goodness we have received
the wine we offer you:
fruit of the vine and work of human hands,
it will become our spiritual drink.

R. Blessed be God for ever.

The Priest completes additional personal preparatory rites, and the people rise as he says:

Pr. Pray, brethren (brothers and sisters),
that my sacrifice and yours
may be acceptable to God,
the almighty Father.

**R. May the Lord accept the sacrifice at your hands
for the praise and glory of his name,
for our good
and the good of all his holy Church.**

Pr: Gepriesen bist du, Herr, unser Gott, Schöpfer der Welt. Du schenkst uns das Brot, die Frucht der Erde und der menschlichen Arbeit. Wir bringen dieses Brot vor dein Angesicht, damit es uns das Brot des Lebens werde.
A: Gepriesen bist du in Ewigkeit, Herr, unser Gott.

Der Priester nimmt den Kelch, hält ihn über den Altar und spricht:
Pr: Gepriesen bist Du, Herr, unser Gott, Schöpfer der Welt. Du schenkst uns den Wein, die Frucht des Weinstocks und der menschlichen Arbeit. Wir bringen diesen Kelch vor dein Angesicht, damit er uns der Kelch des Heiles werde.
A: Gepriesen bist du in Ewigkeit, Herr, unser Gott.

Die Gläubigen stehen; der Priester lädt sie zum Eucharistischen Opfer ein:
Pr: Betet, Brüder und Schwestern,
dass mein und euer Opfer Gott,
dem allmächtigen Vater, gefalle.

**A: Der Herr nehme das Opfer an aus deinen Händen zum Lob und Ruhm seines Namens,
zum Segen für uns und seine ganze heilige Kirche.**

The Prayer over the Offerings

The Priest concludes the Prayer over the Offerings: **R. Amen.**

The Eucharistic Prayer

Extending his hands, the Priest says:

Pr. The Lord be with you.

R. And with your spirit.

Pr. Lift up your hearts.

R. We lift them up to the Lord.

Pr. Let us give thanks to the Lord our God.

R. It is right and just.

At the end of the Preface all sing or say:

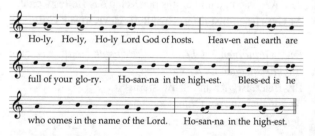

Ho-ly, Ho-ly, Ho-ly Lord God of hosts. Heav-en and earth are full of your glo-ry. Ho-san-na in the high-est. Bless-ed is he who comes in the name of the Lord. Ho-san-na in the high-est.

Holy, Holy, Holy Lord God of hosts.
Heaven and earth are full of your glory.
Hosanna in the highest.
Blessed is he who comes in the name of the Lord.
Hosanna in the highest.

After the Sanctus the congregation kneels.

Der Priester trägt das Gabengebet vor. Die Gläubigen antworten: **Amen.**

Eucharistisches Hochgebet

Pr: Der Herr sei mit euch.

A: Und mit deinem Geiste.

Pr: Erhebet die Herzen.

A: Wir haben sie beim Herrn.

Pr: Lasset uns danken dem Herrn, unserm Gott.

A: Das ist würdig und recht.

Der Priester singt oder spricht die Präfation entsprechend der Zeit im Kirchenjahr bzw. dem (Feier-) Tag. Gemeinsam mit der Gemeinde singt oder spricht er das Sanctus:

Heilig, heilig, heilig Gott,
Herr aller Mächte und Gewalten.
Erfüllt sind Himmel und Erde von deiner Herrlichkeit.
Hosanna in der Höhe.
Hochgelobt sei, der da kommt im Namen des Herrn.
Hosanna in der Höhe.

Eucharistic Prayer I
(The Roman Canon)

Pr. To you, therefore, most merciful Father,
we make humble prayer and petition
through Jesus Christ, your Son, our Lord:
that you accept
and bless ✠ these gifts, these offerings,
these holy and unblemished sacrifices,
which we offer you firstly
for your holy catholic Church.
Be pleased to grant her peace,
to guard, unite and govern her
throughout the whole world,
together with your servant *N.* our Pope and *N.* our Bishop,
and all those who, holding to the truth,
hand on the catholic and apostolic faith.

Remember, Lord, your servants *N.* and *N.*
and all gathered here,
whose faith and devotion are known to you.
For them, we offer you this sacrifice of praise
or they offer it for themselves
and all who are dear to them:
for the redemption of their souls,
in hope of health and well-being,
and paying their homage to you,
the eternal God, living and true.

Eucharistisches Hochgebet I

Pr: Dich, gütiger Vater,
bitten wir durch deinen Sohn, unseren Herrn Jesus
Christus:
Nimm diese heiligen,
makellosen Opfergaben an und ✠ segne sie.

Wir bringen sie dar vor allem für deine heilige katholische
Kirche in Gemeinschaft mit deinem Diener,
unserem Papst *N.*, mit unserem Bischof *N.*
und mit allen,
die Sorge tragen für den rechten,
katholischen und apostolischen Glauben.
Schenke deiner Kirche Frieden und Einheit,
behüte und leite sie auf der ganzen Erde.

Gedenke deiner Diener und Dienerinnen *N.*
(für die wir heute besonders beten) und aller,
die hier versammelt sind.
(Die Gläubigen beten in Stille für die Lebenden.)

Herr, du kennst ihren Glauben und ihre Hingabe;
für sie bringen wir dieses Opfer des Lobes dar,
und sie selber weihen es dir für sich und für alle,
die ihnen verbunden sind,
für ihre Erlösung und für ihre Hoffnung auf das
unverlierbare Heil.
Vor dich, den ewigen, lebendigen und wahren Gott,
bringen sie ihre Gebete und Gaben.

In communion with those whose memory we venerate,
especially the glorious ever-Virgin Mary,
Mother of our God and Lord, Jesus Christ,
and blessed Joseph, her Spouse,
your blessed Apostles and Martyrs,
Peter and Paul, Andrew,
(James, John,
Thomas, James, Philip,
Bartholomew, Matthew,
Simon and Jude;
Linus, Cletus, Clement, Sixtus,
Cornelius, Cyprian,
Lawrence, Chrysogonus,
John and Paul,
Cosmas and Damian)
and all your Saints;
we ask that through their merits and prayers,
in all things we may be defended
by your protecting help.
(Through Christ our Lord. Amen.)

Therefore, Lord, we pray:
graciously accept this oblation of our service,
that of your whole family;
order our days in your peace,
and command that we be delivered
from eternal damnation
and counted among the flock of those you have chosen.
(Through Christ our Lord. Amen.)

Be pleased, O God, we pray,

In Gemeinschaft mit der ganzen Kirche gedenken wir
deiner Heiligen:
Wir ehren vor allem Maria, die glorreiche,
allzeit jungfräuliche Mutter unseres Herrn und Gottes
Jesus Christus.
Wir ehren ihren Bräutigam, den heiligen Josef;
deine heiligen Apostel und Märtyrer:
Petrus und Paulus, Andreas
(Jakobus, Johannes, Tomas, Jakobus, Philippus,
Bartholomäus, Mattäus,
Simon und Taddäus,
Linus, Kletus, Klemens, Xystus,
Kornelius, Cyprianus,
Laurentius, Chrysogonus,
Johannes und Paulus, Kosmas und Damianus)
und alle deine Heiligen; blicke auf ihr heiliges Leben
und Sterben und gewähre uns auf ihre Fürsprache in
allem deine Hilfe und deinen Schutz.

Nimm gnädig an, o Gott,
diese Gaben deiner Diener und deiner ganzen Gemeinde;
ordne unsere Tage in deinem Frieden,
rette uns vor dem ewigen Verderben und nimm uns auf in
die Schar deiner Erwählten.
Schenke, o Gott, diesen Gaben Segen in Fülle und nimm
sie zu eigen an.

to bless, acknowledge,
and approve this offering in every respect;
make it spiritual and acceptable,
so that it may become for us
the Body and Blood of your most beloved Son,
our Lord Jesus Christ.
On the day before he was to suffer,
he took bread in his holy and venerable hands,
and with eyes raised to heaven
to you, O God, his almighty Father,
giving you thanks, he said the blessing,
broke the bread
and gave it to his disciples, saying:

> 'TAKE THIS, ALL OF YOU, AND EAT OF IT,
> FOR THIS IS MY BODY,
> WHICH WILL BE GIVEN UP FOR YOU.'

In a similar way, when supper was ended,
he took this precious chalice
in his holy and venerable hands,
and once more giving you thanks, he said the blessing
and gave the chalice to his disciples, saying:

> 'TAKE THIS, ALL OF YOU, AND DRINK FROM IT,
> FOR THIS IS THE CHALICE OF MY BLOOD,
> THE BLOOD OF THE NEW AND ETERNAL COVENANT,
> WHICH WILL BE POURED OUT FOR YOU AND FOR MANY
> FOR THE FORGIVENESS OF SINS.
>
> DO THIS IN MEMORY OF ME.'

Mache sie uns zum wahren Opfer im Geiste,
das dir wohlgefällt:
zum Leib und Blut deines geliebten Sohnes,
unseres Herrn Jesus Christus.

Am Abend vor seinem Leiden nahm er das Brot in seine
heiligen und ehrwürdigen Hände,
erhob die Augen zum Himmel, zu dir, seinem Vater,
dem allmächtigen Gott, sagte dir Lob und Dank,
brach das Brot, reichte es seinen Jüngern und sprach:

> 'Nehmet und esset alle davon:
> Das ist mein Leib,
> der für euch hingegeben wird.'

Ebenso nahm er nach dem Mahl diesen erhabenen Kelch
in seine heiligen und ehrwürdigen Hände,
sagte dir Lob und Dank,
reichte den Kelch seinen Jüngern und sprach:

> 'Nehmet und trinket alle daraus:
> Das ist der Kelch des neuen und ewigen Bundes,
> mein Blut,
> das für euch und für alle vergossen wird zur
> Vergebung der Sünden.
>
> Tut dies zu meinem Gedächtnis.'

Pr. The mystery of faith.

The people continue, acclaiming one of the following:

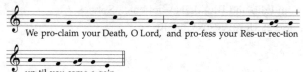

We pro-claim your Death, O Lord, and pro-fess your Res-ur-rec-tion un-til you come a-gain.

1. We proclaim your Death, O Lord,
and profess your Resurrection
until you come again.

When we eat this Bread and drink this Cup, we pro-claim your Death, O Lord, un-til you come a-gain.

2. When we eat this Bread and drink this Cup,
we proclaim your Death, O Lord,
until you come again.

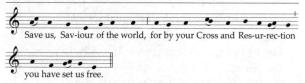

Save us, Sav-iour of the world, for by your Cross and Res-ur-rec-tion you have set us free.

3. Save us, Saviour of the world,
for by your Cross and Resurrection
you have set us free.

Pr: Geheimnis des Glaubens:

**A: Deinen Tod, o Herr,
verkünden wir, und deine Auferstehung preisen wir,
bis du kommst in Herrlichkeit.**

Pr. Therefore, O Lord,
as we celebrate the memorial of the blessed Passion,
the Resurrection from the dead,
and the glorious Ascension into heaven
of Christ, your Son, our Lord,
we, your servants and your holy people,
offer to your glorious majesty
from the gifts that you have given us,
this pure victim,
this holy victim,
this spotless victim,
the holy Bread of eternal life
and the Chalice of everlasting salvation.

Be pleased to look upon these offerings
with a serene and kindly countenance,
and to accept them,
as once you were pleased to accept
the gifts of your servant Abel the just,
the sacrifice of Abraham, our father in faith,
and the offering of your high priest Melchizedek,
a holy sacrifice, a spotless victim.

In humble prayer we ask you, almighty God:
command that these gifts be borne
by the hands of your holy Angel
to your altar on high
in the sight of your divine majesty,
so that all of us, who through this participation at the altar

Pr: Darum, gütiger Vater, feiern wir,
deine Diener und dein heiliges Volk,
das Gedächtnis deines Sohnes,
unseres Herrn Jesus Christus.
Wir verkünden sein heilbringendes Leiden,
seine Auferstehung von den Toten und seine glorreiche
Himmelfahrt.
So bringen wir aus den Gaben,
die du uns geschenkt hast, dir,
dem erhabenen Gott,
die reine,
heilige und makellose Opfergabe dar:
das Brot des Lebens und den Kelch des ewigen Heiles.

Blicke versöhnt und gütig darauf nieder und nimm sie an
wie einst die Gaben deines gerechten Dieners Abel,
wie das Opfer unseres Vaters Abraham,
wie die heilige Gabe,
das reine Opfer deines Hohenpriesters Melchisedech.

Wir bitten dich, allmächtiger Gott:
Dein heiliger Engel trage diese Opfergabe auf deinen
himmlischen Altar vor deine göttliche Herrlichkeit;
und wenn wir durch unsere Teilnahme am Altar den
heiligen Leib und das Blut deines Sohnes empfangen,
erfülle uns mit aller Gnade und allem Segen des Himmels.

Gedenke auch deiner Diener und Dienerinnen *N.* und
N., die uns vorausgegangen sind,

receive the most holy Body and Blood of your Son,
may be filled with every grace and heavenly blessing.
(Through Christ our Lord. Amen.)

Remember also, Lord, your servants *N.* and *N.*,
who have gone before us with the sign of faith
and rest in the sleep of peace.
Grant them, O Lord, we pray,
and all who sleep in Christ,
a place of refreshment, light and peace.
(Through Christ our Lord. Amen.)
To us, also, your servants, who, though sinners,
hope in your abundant mercies,
graciously grant some share
and fellowship with your holy Apostles and Martyrs:
with John the Baptist, Stephen,
Matthias, Barnabas,
(Ignatius, Alexander,
Marcellinus, Peter,
Felicity, Perpetua,
Agatha, Lucy,
Agnes, Cecilia, Anastasia)
and all your Saints;
admit us, we beseech you,
into their company,
not weighing our merits,
but granting us your pardon,
through Christ our Lord.

bezeichnet mit dem Siegel des Glaubens, und die nun
ruhen in Frieden.
(Die Gläubigen beten in Stille für die Verstorbenen.)

Wir bitten dich:
Führe sie und alle, die in Christus entschlafen sind, in das
Land der Verheißung,
des Lichtes und des Friedens.

Auch uns, deinen sündigen Dienern, die auf deine reiche
Barmherzigkeit hoffen,
gib Anteil und Gemeinschaft mit deinen heiligen Aposteln
und Märtyrern:
Johannes, Stephanus,
Mattias, Barnabas
(Ignatius, Alexander,
Marzellinus, Petrus,
Felizitas, Perpetua,
Agatha, Luzia,
Agnes, Cäcilia, Anastasia)
und mit allen deinen Heiligen;
wäge nicht unser Verdienst,
sondern schenke gnädig Verzeihung und gib uns mit ihnen
das Erbe des Himmels.

Darum bitten wir dich durch unseren Herrn Jesus Christus.
Denn durch ihn erschaffst du immerfort all diese guten
Gaben,
gibst ihnen Leben und Weihe und spendest sie uns.

Through whom
you continue to make all these good things, O Lord;
you sanctify them, fill them with life,
bless them, and bestow them upon us.
The Priest takes the chalice and the paten with the host:
Pr. Through him, and with him, and in him,
O God, almighty Father,
in the unity of the Holy Spirit,
all glory and honour is yours,
for ever and ever.
R. Amen.
Then follows the Communion Rite, p.66.

Eucharistic Prayer II

Pr. The Lord be with you.
R. And with your spirit.
Pr. Lift up your hearts.
R. We lift them up to the Lord.
Pr. Let us give thanks to the Lord our God.
R. It is right and just.
Pr. It is truly right and just, our duty and our salvation,
always and everywhere to give you thanks, Father most holy,
through your beloved Son, Jesus Christ,
your Word through whom you made all things,
whom you sent as our Saviour and Redeemer,
incarnate by the Holy Spirit and born of the Virgin.

Durch ihn und mit ihm und in ihm ist dir, Gott,
allmächtiger Vater,
in der Einheit des Heiligen Geistes alle Herrlichkeit und
Ehre jetzt und in Ewigkeit!

A: Amen.
Die Messe wird fortgesetzt mit dem Kommunion-Ritus auf
Seite. 67.

Eucharistisches Hochgebet II

Pr: Der Herr sei mit euch.
A: Und mit deinem Geiste.
Pr: Erhebet die Herzen.
A: Wir haben sie beim Herrn.
Pr: Lasset uns danken dem Herrn, unserm Gott.
A: Das ist würdig und recht.
P. In Wahrheit ist es würdig und recht, dir, Herr,
heiliger Vater, immer und überall zu danken durch
deinen geliebten Sohn Jesus Christus. Er ist dein
Wort, durch ihn hast du alles erschaffen. Ihn hast du
gesandt als unseren Erlöser und Heiland. Er ist

Fulfilling your will and gaining for you a holy people,
he stretched out his hands as he endured his Passion,
so as to break the bonds of death and manifest the
    resurrection.

And so, with the Angels and all the Saints
we declare your glory,
as with one voice we acclaim:
The people sing or say aloud the Sanctus as on p. 26.
Pr. You are indeed Holy, O Lord,
the fount of all holiness.
Make holy, therefore, these gifts, we pray,
by sending down your Spirit upon them like the dewfall,
so that they may become for us
the Body and ✠ Blood of our Lord Jesus Christ.

At the time he was betrayed
and entered willingly into his Passion,
he took bread and, giving thanks, broke it,
and gave it to his disciples, saying:

> 'TAKE THIS, ALL OF YOU, AND EAT OF IT,
> FOR THIS IS MY BODY,
> WHICH WILL BE GIVEN UP FOR YOU.'

In a similar way, when supper was ended,
he took the chalice
and, once more giving thanks,
he gave it to his disciples, saying:

Mensch geworden durch den Heiligen Geist, geboren
von der Jungfrau Maria. Um deinen Ratschluss zu
erfüllen und dir ein heiliges Volk zu erwerben, hat er
sterbend die Arme ausgebreitet am Holze des
Kreuzes. Er hat die Macht des Todes gebrochen und
die Auferstehung kundgetan. Darum preisen wir dich
mit allen Engeln und Heiligen und singen vereint mit
ihnen das Lob deiner Herrlichkeit:
Sanktus S. 27.
Pr: Ja, du bist heilig, großer Gott,
du bist der Quell aller Heiligkeit.
Darum bitten wir dich:
Sende deinen Geist auf diese Gaben herab und heilige sie,
damit sie uns werden Leib und Blut deines Sohnes,
unseres Herrn Jesus Christus.

Denn am Abend, an dem er ausgeliefert wurde und sich
aus freiem Willen dem Leiden unterwarf,
nahm er das Brot und sagte Dank,
brach es, reichte es seinen Jüngern und sprach:

> 'NEHMET UND ESSET ALLE DAVON:
> DAS IST MEIN LEIB,
> DER FÜR EUCH HINGEGEBEN WIRD.'

Ebenso nahm er nach dem Mahl den Kelch,
dankte wiederum,
reichte ihn seinen Jüngern und sprach:

'TAKE THIS, ALL OF YOU, AND DRINK FROM IT,
FOR THIS IS THE CHALICE OF MY BLOOD,
THE BLOOD OF THE NEW AND ETERNAL COVENANT,
WHICH WILL BE POURED OUT FOR YOU AND FOR MANY
FOR THE FORGIVENESS OF SINS.

DO THIS IN MEMORY OF ME.'

Pr. The mystery of faith.
The people continue with one of the acclamations p. 67.
Pr. Therefore, as we celebrate
the memorial of his Death and Resurrection,
we offer you, Lord,
the Bread of life and the Chalice of salvation,
giving thanks that you have held us worthy
to be in your presence and minister to you.
Humbly we pray
that, partaking of the Body and Blood of Christ,
we may be gathered into one by the Holy Spirit.

Remember, Lord, your Church,
spread throughout the world,
and bring her to the fullness of charity,
together with *N.* our Pope and *N.* our Bishop
and all the clergy.

'NEHMET UND TRINKET ALLE DARAUS:
DAS IST DER KELCH DES NEUEN UND EWIGEN BUNDES,
MEIN BLUT,
DAS FÜR EUCH UND FÜR ALLE VERGOSSEN WIRD ZUR
VERGEBUNG DER SÜNDEN.

TUT DIES ZU MEINEM GEDÄCHTNIS.'

Pr: Geheimnis des Glaubens:

Pr: Darum, gütiger Vater,
feiern wir das Gedächtnis des Todes und der Auferstehung
deines Sohnes und bringen dir so das Brot des Lebens und
den Kelch des Heiles dar.
Wir danken dir, dass du uns berufen hast,
vor dir zu stehen und dir zu dienen.
Wir bitten dich:
Schenke uns Anteil an Christi Leib und Blut und lass uns
eins werden durch den Heiligen Geist.

Gedenke deiner Kirche auf der ganzen Erde und vollende
dein Volk in der Liebe,
vereint mit unserem Papst *N.*, unserem Bischof *N.*
und allen Bischöfen,
unseren Priestern und Diakonen und mit allen,
die zum Dienst in der Kirche bestellt sind.

In Masses for the Dead, the following may be added:
Remember your servant *N.*,
whom you have called (today)
from this world to yourself.
Grant that he (she) who was united with your Son
    in a death like his,
may also be one with him in his Resurrection.

Remember also our brothers and sisters
who have fallen asleep in the hope of the resurrection,
and all who have died in your mercy:
welcome them into the light of your face.
Have mercy on us all, we pray,
that with the Blessed Virgin Mary, Mother of God,
with the blessed Apostles,
and all the Saints who have pleased you throughout the ages,
we may merit to be coheirs to eternal life,
and may praise and glorify you
through your Son, Jesus Christ.
The Priest takes the chalice and the paten with the host:
Through him, and with him, and in him,
O God, almighty Father,
in the unity of the Holy Spirit,
all glory and honour is yours,
for ever and ever.
R. Amen.
Then follows the Communion Rite, p. 66.

Gedenke (aller) unserer Brüder und Schwestern,
die entschlafen sind in der Hoffnung, dass sie
auferstehen. Nimm sie und alle, die in deiner Gnade aus
dieser Welt geschieden sind,
in dein Reich auf, wo sie dich schauen von Angesicht zu
Angesicht.

Vater, erbarme dich über uns alle, damit uns das ewige
Leben zuteil wird in der Gemeinschaft mit der seligen
Jungfrau und Gottesmutter Maria,
mit deinen Aposteln und mit allen,
die bei dir Gnade gefunden haben von Anbeginn der Welt,
dass wir dich loben und preisen durch deinen Sohn Jesus
Christus.

Durch ihn und mit ihm und in ihm ist dir, Gott, allmächtiger
Vater, in der Einheit des Heiligen Geistes alle Herrlichkeit
und Ehre jetzt und in Ewigkeit!

A: Amen.

*Die Messe wird fortgesetzt mit dem Kommunion-Ritus auf
Seite. 67.*

Eucharistic Prayer III

Pr. You are indeed Holy, O Lord,
and all you have created
rightly gives you praise,
for through your Son our Lord Jesus Christ,
by the power and working of the Holy Spirit,
you give life to all things and make them holy,
and you never cease to gather a people to yourself,
so that from the rising of the sun to its setting
a pure sacrifice may be offered to your name.

Therefore, O Lord, we humbly implore you:
by the same Spirit graciously make holy
these gifts we have brought to you for consecration,
that they may become the Body and ✠ Blood
of your Son our Lord Jesus Christ,
at whose command we celebrate these mysteries.

For on the night he was betrayed
he himself took bread,
and, giving you thanks, he said the blessing,
broke the bread and gave it to his disciples, saying:

'TAKE THIS, ALL OF YOU,
AND EAT OF IT, FOR THIS IS MY BODY,
WHICH WILL BE GIVEN UP FOR YOU.'

In a similar way, when supper was ended,
he took the chalice,
and, giving you thanks, he said the blessing,
and gave the chalice to his disciples, saying:

Eucharistisches Hochgebet III

Pr: Ja, du bist heilig, großer Gott,
und alle deine Werke verkünden dein Lob.
Denn durch deinen Sohn, unseren Herrn Jesus
Christus,
und in der Kraft des Heiligen Geistes erfüllst du die
ganze Schöpfung mit Leben und Gnade.
Bis ans Ende der Zeiten versammelst du dir ein Volk,
damit deinem Namen das reine Opfer dargebracht
werde vom Aufgang der Sonne bis zum Untergang.

Darum bitten wir dich, allmächtiger Gott:
Heilige unsere Gaben durch deinen Geist,
damit sie uns werden Leib und Blut deines Sohnes,
unseres Herrn Jesus Christus,
der uns aufgetragen hat,
dieses Geheimnis zu feiern.

Denn in der Nacht, da er verraten wurde, nahm er das
Brot und sagte Dank, brach es, reichte es seinen Jüngern
und sprach:

'NEHMET UND ESSET ALLE DAVON:
DAS IST MEIN LEIB,
DER FÜR EUCH HINGEGEBEN WIRD.'

Ebenso nahm er nach dem Mahl den Kelch,
dankte wiederum,
reichte ihn seinen Jüngern und sprach:

'TAKE THIS, ALL OF YOU, AND DRINK FROM IT,
FOR THIS IS THE CHALICE OF MY BLOOD
THE BLOOD OF THE NEW AND ETERNAL COVENANT,
WHICH WILL BE POURED OUT FOR YOU AND FOR MANY
FOR THE FORGIVENESS OF SINS.

DO THIS IN MEMORY OF ME.'

Pr. The mystery of faith.
The people continue with one of the acclamations, p. 34.
Pr. Therefore, O Lord, as we celebrate the memorial
of the saving Passion of your Son,
his wondrous Resurrection
and Ascension into heaven,
and as we look forward to his second coming,
we offer you in thanksgiving
this holy and living sacrifice.

Look, we pray, upon the oblation of your Church
and, recognizing the sacrificial Victim by whose death
you willed to reconcile us to yourself,
grant that we, who are nourished
by the Body and Blood of your Son
and filled with his Holy Spirit,
may become one body, one spirit in Christ.

May he make of us
an eternal offering to you,
so that we may obtain an inheritance with your elect,

'Nehmet und trinket alle daraus:

Das ist der Kelch des neuen und ewigen Bundes,
mein Blut,

das für euch und für alle vergossen wird zur
Vergebung der Sünden.

Tut dies zu meinem Gedächtnis.'

Pr: Geheimnis des Glaubens:
A: Deinen Tod, o Herr... S. 35
Pr: Darum, gütiger Vater, feiern wir das Gedächtnis
deines Sohnes:
Wir verkünden sein heilbringendes Leiden,
seine glorreiche Auferstehung und Himmelfahrt und
erwarten seine Wiederkunft.
So bringen wir dir mit Lob und Dank dieses heilige und
lebendige Opfer dar.
Schau gütig auf die Gabe deiner Kirche.
Denn sie stellt dir das Lamm vor Augen, das geopfert
wurde und uns nach deinem Willen mit dir versöhnt hat.
Stärke uns durch den Leib und das Blut deines Sohnes und
erfülle uns mit seinem Heiligen Geist,
damit wir ein Leib und ein Geist werden in Christus.

Er mache uns auf immer zu einer Gabe,
die dir wohlgefällt, damit wir das verheißene Erbe
erlangen mit deinen Auserwählten,
mit der seligen Jungfrau und Gottesmutter Maria,

especially with the most Blessed Virgin Mary,
  Mother of God,
with your blessed Apostles and glorious Martyrs
(with Saint *N.: the Saint of the day or Patron Saint*)
and with all the Saints,
on whose constant intercession in your presence
we rely for unfailing help.

May this Sacrifice of our reconciliation,
we pray, O Lord,
advance the peace and salvation of all the world.
Be pleased to confirm in faith and charity
your pilgrim Church on earth,
with your servant *N.* our Pope and *N.* our Bishop,
the Order of Bishops, all the clergy,
and the entire people you have gained for your own.

Listen graciously to the prayers of this family,
whom you have summoned before you:
in your compassion, O merciful Father,
gather to yourself all your children
scattered throughout the world.

† To our departed brothers and sisters
and to all who were pleasing to you
at their passing from this life,
give kind admittance to your kingdom.
There we hope to enjoy for ever the fullness of your glory
through Christ our Lord,
through whom you bestow on the world all that is good.†

mit deinen Aposteln und Märtyrern,
mit dem - der - heiligen *N.: (Tagesheiliger oder Patron)*
und mit allen Heiligen, auf deren Fürsprache wir vertrauen.

Barmherziger Gott, wir bitten dich:
Dieses Opfer unserer Versöhnung bringe der ganzen Welt
Frieden und Heil.
Beschütze deine Kirche auf ihrem Weg durch die Zeit
und stärke sie im Glauben und in der Liebe: deinen
Diener, unseren Papst *N.*, unseren Bischof *N.*
und die Gemeinschaft der Bischöfe,
unsere Priester und Diakone, alle, die zum Dienst in der
Kirche bestellt sind,
und das ganze Volk deiner Erlösten.

Erhöre, gütiger Vater, die Gebete der hier versammelten
Gemeinde und führe zu dir auch alle deine Söhne und
Töchter,
die noch fern sind von dir.
Erbarme dich (aller) unserer verstorbenen Brüder und
Schwestern und aller,
die in deiner Gnade aus dieser Welt geschieden sind.
Nimm sie auf in deine Herrlichkeit.
Und mit ihnen lass auch uns,
wie du verheißen hast,
zu Tische sitzen in deinem Reich.
Darum bitten wir dich durch unseren Herrn Jesus Christus.
Denn durch ihn schenkst du der Welt alle guten Gaben.

The Priest takes the chalice and the paten with the host:
Through him, and with him, and in him,
O God, almighty Father,
in the unity of the Holy Spirit,
all glory and honour is yours,
for ever and ever.
R. Amen.
Then follows the Communion Rite, p. 66.

When this Eucharistic Prayer is used in Masses for the Dead, the following may be said:
† Remember your servant *N.*
whom you have called (today)
from this world to yourself.
Grant that he (she) who was united with your Son
    in a death like his,
may also be one with him in his Resurrection,
when from the earth
he will raise up in the flesh those who have died,
and transform our lowly body
after the pattern of his own glorious body.
To our departed brothers and sisters, too,
and to all who were pleasing to you
at their passing from this life,
give kind admittance to your kingdom.
There we hope to enjoy for ever the fullness of your glory,
when you will wipe away every tear from our eyes.

Durch ihn und mit ihm und in ihm ist dir, Gott,
allmächtiger Vater,
in der Einheit des Heiligen Geistes
alle Herrlichkeit und Ehre jetzt und in Ewigkeit!

A: Amen.

Die Messe wird fortgesetzt mit dem Kommunion-Ritus auf Seite. 67.

For seeing you, our God, as you are,
we shall be like you for all the ages
and praise you without end, (*He joins his hands.*)
through Christ our Lord,
through whom you bestow on the world all that is good.†

Eucharistic Prayer IV

Pr. The Lord be with you.
R. And with your spirit.
Pr. Lift up your hearts.
R. We lift them up to the Lord.
Pr. Let us give thanks to the Lord our God.
R. It is right and just.
Pr. It is truly right to give you thanks,
truly just to give you glory, Father most holy,
for you are the one God living and true,
existing before all ages and abiding for all eternity,
dwelling in unapproachable light;
yet you, who alone are good, the source of life,
have made all that is,
so that you might fill your creatures with blessings
and bring joy to many of them by the glory of your light.

And so, in your presence are countless hosts of Angels,
who serve you day and night
and, gazing upon the glory of your face,
glorify you without ceasing.

Eucharistisches Hochgebet IV

Pr: Der Herr sei mit euch.

A: Und mit deinem Geiste.

Pr: Erhebet die Herzen.

A: Wir haben sie beim Herrn.

P. In Wahrheit ist es würdig, dir zu danken, heiliger Vater. Es ist recht, dich zu preisen. Denn du allein bist der lebendige und wahre Gott. Du bist vor den Zeiten und lebst in Ewigkeit. Du wohnst in unzugänglichem Lichte. Alles hast du erschaffen, denn du bist die Liebe und der Ursprung des Lebens. Du erfüllst deine Geschöpfe mit Segen und erfreust sie alle mit dem Glanz deines Lichtes. Vor dir stehen die Scharen der Engel und schauen dein Angesicht. Sie dienen dir Tag und Nacht, nie endet ihr Lobgesang. Mit ihnen preisen auch wir deinen Namen, durch unseren Mund rühmen dich alle Geschöpfe und künden voll Freude das Lob deiner Herrlichkeit:

With them we, too, confess your name in exultation,
giving voice to every creature under heaven,
as we acclaim:
The people sing or say aloud the Sanctus as on p. 26.
Pr. We give you praise, Father most holy,
for you are great
and you have fashioned all your works
in wisdom and in love.
You formed man in your own image
and entrusted the whole world to his care,
so that in serving you alone, the Creator,
he might have dominion over all creatures.
And when through disobedience he had lost your friendship,
you did not abandon him to the domain of death.
For you came in mercy to the aid of all,
so that those who seek might find you.
Time and again you offered them covenants
and through the prophets
taught them to look forward to salvation.

And you so loved the world, Father most holy,
that in the fullness of time
you sent your Only Begotten Son to be our Saviour.
Made incarnate by the Holy Spirit
and born of the Virgin Mary,
he shared our human nature
in all things but sin.

Sanktus S. 27.

Pr: Wir preisen dich, heiliger Vater,
denn groß bist du, und alle deine Werke künden deine
Weisheit und Liebe.
Den Menschen hast du nach deinem Bild geschaffen
und ihm die Sorge für die ganze Welt anvertraut.
Über alle Geschöpfe sollte er herrschen und allein dir,
seinem Schöpfer, dienen.
Als er im Ungehorsam deine Freundschaft verlor und
der Macht des Todes verfiel,
hast du ihn dennoch nicht verlassen,
sondern voll Erbarmen allen geholfen,
dich zu suchen und zu finden.

Immer wieder hast du den Menschen deinen Bund
angeboten und sie durch die Propheten gelehrt,
das Heil zu erwarten.
So sehr hast du die Welt geliebt, heiliger Vater,
dass du deinen eingeborenen Sohn als Retter gesandt
hast, nachdem die Fülle der Zeiten gekommen war.

Er ist Mensch geworden durch den Heiligen Geist,
geboren von der Jungfrau Maria.
Er hat wie wir als Mensch gelebt,
in allem uns gleich außer der Sünde.

To the poor he proclaimed the good news of salvation,
to prisoners, freedom,
and to the sorrowful of heart, joy.
To accomplish your plan,
he gave himself up to death,
and, rising from the dead,
he destroyed death and restored life.

And that we might live no longer for ourselves
but for him who died and rose again for us,
he sent the Holy Spirit from you, Father,
as the first fruits for those who believe,
so that, bringing to perfection his work in the world,
he might sanctify creation to the full.

Therefore, O Lord, we pray:
may this same Holy Spirit
graciously sanctify these offerings,
that they may become
the Body and ✠ Blood of our Lord Jesus Christ
for the celebration of this great mystery,
which he himself left us
as an eternal covenant.

For when the hour had come
for him to be glorified by you, Father most holy,
having loved his own who were in the world,
he loved them to the end:
and while they were at supper,
he took bread, blessed and broke it,
and gave it to his disciples, saying:

Den Armen verkündete er die Botschaft vom Heil,
den Gefangenen Freiheit, den Trauernden Freude.

Um deinen Ratschluss zu erfüllen,
hat er sich dem Tod überliefert,
durch seine Auferstehung den Tod bezwungen und das
Leben neu geschaffen.

Damit wir nicht mehr uns selber leben, sondern ihm, der
für uns gestorben und auferstanden ist,
hat er von dir, Vater, als erste Gabe für alle, die glauben,
den Heiligen Geist gesandt,
der das Werk deines Sohnes auf Erden weiterführt und
alle Heiligung vollendet.

So bitten wir dich, Vater:
der Geist heilige diese Gaben,
damit sie uns werden Leib und Blut unseres Herrn Jesus
Christus,
der uns die Feier dieses Geheimnisses aufgetragen hat
als Zeichen des ewigen Bundes.
Da er die Seinen liebte,
die in der Welt waren,
liebte er sie bis zur Vollendung.

Und als die Stunde kam,
da er von Dir verherrlicht werden sollte,
nahm er beim Mahl das Brot und sagte Dank,
brach das Brot,
reichte es seinen Jüngern und sprach:

'TAKE THIS, ALL OF YOU, AND EAT OF IT,
FOR THIS IS MY BODY,
WHICH WILL BE GIVEN UP FOR YOU.'

In a similar way,
taking the chalice filled with the fruit of the vine,
he gave thanks,
and gave the chalice to his disciples, saying:

'TAKE THIS, ALL OF YOU, AND DRINK FROM IT,
FOR THIS IS THE CHALICE OF MY BLOOD,
THE BLOOD OF THE NEW AND ETERNAL COVENANT,
WHICH WILL BE POURED OUT FOR YOU AND FOR MANY
FOR THE FORGIVENESS OF SINS.

DO THIS IN MEMORY OF ME.'

Pr. The mystery of faith.
The people continue with one of the acclamations, p. 34.
Pr. Therefore, O Lord,
as we now celebrate the memorial of our redemption,
we remember Christ's Death
and his descent to the realm of the dead,
we proclaim his Resurrection
and his Ascension to your right hand,
and, as we await his coming in glory,
we offer you his Body and Blood,
the sacrifice acceptable to you
which brings salvation to the whole world.

Look, O Lord, upon the Sacrifice

'NEHMET UND ESSET ALLE DAVON:
DAS IST MEIN LEIB,
DER FÜR EUCH HINGEGEBEN WIRD.'

Ebenso nahm er den Kelch mit Wein,
dankte wiederum,
reichte den Kelch seinen Jüngern und sprach:

'NEHMET UND TRINKET ALLE DARAUS:
DAS IST DER KELCH DES NEUEN UND EWIGEN BUNDES,
MEIN BLUT,
DAS FÜR EUCH UND FÜR ALLE VERGOSSEN WIRD ZUR
VERGEBUNG DER SÜNDEN.

TUT DIES ZU MEINEM GEDÄCHTNIS.'

Pr: Geheimnis des Glaubens.
**A: Deinen Tod, o Herr, verkünden wir, und deine
Auferstehung preisen wir, bis du kommst in Herrlichkeit.**
Pr: Darum, gütiger Vater, feiern wir das Gedächtnis
unserer Erlösung.
Wir verkünden den Tod deines Sohnes und sein
Hinabsteigen zu den Vätern,
bekennen seine Auferstehung und Himmelfahrt und
erwarten sein Kommen in Herrlichkeit.
So bringen wir dir seinen Leib und sein Blut dar,
das Opfer,
das dir wohlgefällt und der ganzen Welt Heil bringt.

Sieh her auf die Opfergabe,
die du selber deiner Kirche bereitet hast, und gib,

which you yourself have provided for your Church,
and grant in your loving kindness
to all who partake of this one Bread and one Chalice
that, gathered into one body by the Holy Spirit,
they may truly become a living sacrifice in Christ
to the praise of your glory.

Therefore, Lord, remember now
all for whom we offer this sacrifice:
especially your servant *N.* our Pope,
N. our Bishop, and the whole Order of Bishops,
all the clergy,
those who take part in this offering,
those gathered here before you,
your entire people,
and all who seek you with a sincere heart.

Remember also
those who have died in the peace of your Christ
and all the dead,
whose faith you alone have known.

To all of us, your children,
grant, O merciful Father,
that we may enter into a heavenly inheritance
with the Blessed Virgin Mary, Mother of God,
and with your Apostles and Saints in your kingdom.
There, with the whole of creation,
freed from the corruption of sin and death,
may we glorify you through Christ our Lord,
through whom you bestow on the world all that is good.

dass alle, die Anteil erhalten an dem einen Brot und dem
einen Kelch,
ein Leib werden im Heiligen Geist,
eine lebendige Opfergabe in Christus zum Lob deiner
Herrlichkeit.

Herr, gedenke aller, für deren Heil wir das Opfer
darbringen. Wir bitten dich für unseren Papst *N.*,
unseren Bischof *N.* und die Gemeinschaft der Bischöfe,
für unsere Priester und Diakone und für alle,
die zum Dienst in der Kirche bestellt sind, für alle,
die ihre Gaben spenden, für die hier versammelte
Gemeinde, für dein ganzes Volk und für alle Menschen,
die mit lauterem Herzen dich suchen.

Wir empfehlen dir auch jene,
die im Frieden Christi heimgegangen sind,
und alle Verstorbenen, um deren Glauben niemand weiß
als du.

Gütiger Vater, gedenke dass wir deine Kinder sind, und
schenke uns allen das Erbe des Himmels in Gemeinschaft
mit der seligen Jungfrau und Gottesmutter Maria, mit
deinen Aposteln und mit allen Heiligen.
Und wenn die ganze Schöpfung von der Verderbnis der
Sünde und des Todes befreit ist, lass uns zusammen mit
ihr dich verherrlichen in deinem Reich durch unseren
Herrn Jesus Christus.
Denn durch ihn schenkst du der Welt alle guten Gaben.

The Priest takes the chalice and the paten with the host:
Through him, and with him, and in him,
O God, almighty Father,
in the unity of the Holy Spirit,
all glory and honour is yours,
for ever and ever. **R. Amen.**

THE COMMUNION RITE

*Eating and drinking together the Lord's Body and Blood
in a paschal meal is the culmination of the Eucharist.*

The Lord's Prayer

*After the chalice and paten have been set down, the
congregation stands and the Priest says:*
Pr. At the Saviour's command
and formed by divine teaching,
we dare to say:
Together with the people, he continues:
**Our Father, who art in heaven,
hallowed be thy name;
thy kingdom come,
thy will be done
on earth as it is in heaven.
Give us this day our daily bread,
and forgive us our trespasses,
as we forgive those who trespass against us;
and lead us not into temptation,
but deliver us from evil.**

Durch ihn und mit ihm und in ihm ist dir, Gott,
allmächtiger Vater,
in der Einheit des Heiligen Geistes
alle Herrlichkeit und Ehre jetzt und in Ewigkeit!

A: Amen.

DER KOMMUNION-RITUS

Das Vaterunser

Der Priester betet mit den Gläubigen:

Pr: Lasset uns beten, wie der Herr uns zu beten gelehrt hat.

**A: Vater unser im Himmel,
geheiligt werde dein Name,
dein Reich komme,
dein Wille geschehe wie im Himmel,
so auch auf Erden.
Unser tägliches Brot gib uns heute und vergib uns
unsere Schuld,
wie auch wir vergeben unseren Schuldigern.
Und führe uns nicht in Versuchung,
sondern erlöse uns von dem Bösen. Amen.**

Pr. Deliver us, Lord, we pray, from every evil,
graciously grant peace in our days,
that, by the help of your mercy,
we may be always free from sin
and safe from all distress,
as we await the blessed hope
and the coming of our Saviour, Jesus Christ.
R. For the kingdom,
the power and the glory are yours
now and for ever.

The Peace

Pr. Lord Jesus Christ,
who said to your Apostles:
Peace I leave you, my peace I give you;
look not on our sins,
but on the faith of your Church,
and graciously grant her peace and unity
in accordance with your will.
Who live and reign for ever and ever.
R. Amen.

Pr. The peace of the Lord be with you always.
R. And with your spirit.

Then the Deacon, or the Priest, adds:

Pr. Let us offer each other the sign of peace.
And all offer one another the customary sign of peace.

Pr: Erlöse uns, Herr, allmächtiger Vater,
von allem Bösen und gib Frieden in unseren Tagen.
Komm uns zu Hilfe mit deinem Erbarmen und bewahre
uns vor Verwirrung und Sünde,
damit wir voll Zuversicht das Kommen unseres
Erlösers Jesus Christus erwarten.
Die Gläubigen antworten:
**A: Denn dein ist das Reich und die Kraft und die
Herrlichkeit in Ewigkeit.**
Amen.
*Der Priester lädt nun mit folgenden oder ähnlichen
Worten zum Friedensgebet ein:*
Pr: Der Herr hat zu seinen Aposteln gesagt:
Frieden hinterlasse ich euch,
meinen Frieden gebe ich euch.
Deshalb bitten wir:
Herr Jesus Christus, schau nicht auf unsere Sünden,
sondern auf den Glauben deiner Kirche und schenke ihr
nach deinem Willen Einheit und Frieden.
Pr: Der Friede des Herrn sei allezeit mit euch.
A: Und mit deinem Geiste.

Pr: (oder Diakon). Gebt einander ein Zeichen des
Friedens und der Versöhnung.
*Die Gläubigen tauschen - entsprechend der örtlichen
Gewohnheiten - den Friedensgruß aus.*

Breaking of the Bread

Then the Priest takes the host, breaks it over the paten, and places a small piece in the chalice, saying quietly:

Pr. May this mingling of the Body and Blood
of our Lord Jesus Christ
bring eternal life to us who receive it.

Meanwhile the following is sung or said:

**Lamb of God, you take away the sins of the world,
have mercy on us.**

**Lamb of God, you take away the sins of the world,
have mercy on us.**

**Lamb of God, you take away the sins of the world,
grant us peace.**

Invitation to Communion

All kneel; The Priest genuflects, takes the host and, holding it slightly raised above the paten or above the chalice says aloud:

Pr. Behold the Lamb of God,
behold him who takes away the sins of the world.
Blessed are those called to the supper of the Lamb.

**R. Lord, I am not worthy
that you should enter under my roof,
but only say the word
and my soul shall be healed.**

While the Priest is receiving the Body of Christ, the Communion Chant begins.

Der Priester bricht die Hostie über der Schale. Inzwischen wird der Gesang zur Brechung (Agnus Dei) gesungen bzw. gesprochen:

Lamm Gottes, du nimmst hinweg die Sünde der Welt:
erbarme dich unser.
Lamm Gottes, du nimmst hinweg die Sünde der Welt:
erbarme dich unser.
Lamm Gottes, du nimmst hinweg die Sünde der Welt:
gib uns deinen Frieden.

Die Gläubigen knien. Der Priester macht eine Kniebeuge, erhebt die Hostie und sagt:

Pr: Seht das Lamm Gottes, das hinwegnimmt die Sünde der Welt.
Gemeinsam mit den Gläubigen spricht der Priester:
A: Herr, ich bin nicht würdig,
dass du eingehst unter mein Dach,
aber sprich nur ein Wort,
so wird meine Seele gesund.
Jetzt folgt die Kommunion-Antiphon.

Communion Procession

After the priest has reverently consumed the Body and Blood of Christ he takes the paten or ciborium and approaches the communicants.

The Priest raises a host slightly and shows it to each of the communicants, saying:

Pr. The Body of Christ.

R. Amen.

When Communion is ministered from the chalice:

Pr. The Blood of Christ.

R. Amen.

After the distribution of Communion, if appropriate, a sacred silence may be observed for a while, or a psalm or other canticle of praise or a hymn may be sung. Then, the Priest says:

Pr. Let us pray.

Prayer after Communion

All stand and pray in silence for a while, unless silence has just been observed. Then the Priest says the Prayer after Communion, at the end of which the people acclaim:

R. Amen.

Der Priester spricht zu jedem Kommunikanten:

Pr: Der Leib Christi.
A: Amen.
Wenn der Kelch gereicht wird:
Pr: Das Blut Christi.
A: Amen.
Nach der Kommunionausteilung kann der Priester an seinem Sitz eine Weile in stillem Gebet verweilen, während die Gläubigen ihr Dankgebet leise fortführen. Dann spricht der Priester, am Altar oder an seinem Sitz stehend:
Pr: Lasset uns beten.

Am Ende des Gebetes:

A: Amen.

THE CONCLUDING RITES

The Mass closes, sending the faithful forth to put what they have celebrated into effect in their daily lives.

Any brief announcements follow here. Then the dismissal takes place.

Pr. The Lord be with you.

R. And with your spirit.

The Priest blesses the people, saying:

Pr. May almighty God bless you,

the Father, and the Son, and the Holy Spirit.

R. Amen.

Then the Deacon, or the Priest himself says the Dismissal:

Pr. Go forth, the Mass is ended.

R. Thanks be to God. *Or:*

Pr. Go and announce the Gospel of the Lord.

R. Thanks be to God. *Or:*

Pr. Go in peace, glorifying the Lord by your life.

R. Thanks be to God. *Or:*

Pr. Go in peace.

R. Thanks be to God.

Then the Priest venerates the altar as at the beginning. After making a profound bow with the ministers, he withdraws.

DER ABSCHLUSSRITUS

Wenn noch kurze Verlautbarungen zu machen sind, werden sie hier eingefügt.

Pr: Der Herr sei mit euch.
A: Und mit deinem Geiste.

Pr: Es segne euch der allmächtige Gott, der Vater und der Sohn und der Heilige Geist.
A: Amen.
Der Priester entlässt die Gläubigen mit den Worten:
Pr: Gehet hin in Frieden.
A: Dank sei Gott, dem Herrn.

COMMON PRAYERS

The Benedictus

Blessed be the Lord, the God of Israel!
He has visited his people and redeemed them.

    He has raised up for us a mighty saviour
    in the house of David his servant,
    as he promised by the lips of holy men,
    those who his prophets from of old.

A saviour who would free us from our foes,
from the hands of all who hate us.
So his love for our fathers is fulfilled
and his holy covenant remembered.

    He swore to Abraham our father to grant us,
    that free from fear, and saved
    from the hands of our foes,
    we might serve him in holiness and justice
    all the days of our life in his presence.

As for you little child,
you shall be called a prophet of God, the Most High.
You shall go ahead of the Lord
to prepare a way for him,

    To make known to his people their salvation,
    through forgiveness of all their sins,
    the loving kindness of the heart of our God
    who visits us like the dawn from on high.

He will give light to those in darkness,
those who dwell in the shadow of death,
and guide us into the way of peace. (*Lk* 1:68-79)

——— Gebräuchliche Gebete ———

Benedictus

Gepriesen sei der Herr, der Gott Israels!
Denn er hat sein Volk besucht
und ihm Erlösung geschaffen;
er hat uns einen starken Retter erweckt
im Hause seines Knechtes David.
So hat er verheißen von alters her
durch den Mund seiner heiligen Propheten.
Er hat uns errettet vor unsern Feinden
und aus der Hand aller, die uns hassen;
er hat das Erbarmen mit den Vätern an uns vollendet
und an seinen heiligen Bund gedacht, an den Eid,
den er unserm Vater Abraham geschworen hat;
er hat uns geschenkt, dass wir, aus Feindeshand befreit,
ihm furchtlos dienen in Heiligkeit und Gerechtigkeit
vor seinem Angesicht all unsre Tage.
Und du, Kind, wirst Prophet des Höchsten heißen;
denn du wirst dem Herrn vorangehn
und ihm den Weg bereiten.
Du wirst sein Volk mit der Erfahrung des Heils beschenken
in der Vergebung der Sünden.
Durch die barmherzige Liebe unseres Gottes
wird uns besuchen das aufstrahlende Licht aus der Höhe,
um allen zu leuchten, die in Finsternis sitzen
und im Schatten des Todes,
und unsre Schritte zu lenken auf den Weg des Friedens.
(*Lukas* 1,68-79)

The Angelus

May be said morning, noon, and night, to put us in mind that God the Son became man for our salvation.

V. The Angel of the Lord declared to Mary:

R. And she conceived of the Holy Spirit.
    Hail Mary...

V. Behold the handmaid of the Lord:

R. Be it done to me according to your word.
    Hail Mary...

V. And the Word was made Flesh:

R. And dwelt among us.
    Hail Mary...

V. Pray for us, O holy Mother of God.

R. That we may be made worthy of the promises of Christ.

Let us pray:

Pour forth, we beseech you, O Lord, your grace into our hearts, that we, to whom the Incarnation of Christ, your Son, was made known by the message of an angel, may by his passion and cross ✠ be brought to the glory of his resurrection, through the same Christ our Lord. **R. Amen.**

Magnificat

My soul glorifies the Lord,
my spirit rejoices in God, my Saviour.
He looks on his servant in her lowliness;
henceforth all ages will call me blessed.

   The Almighty works marvels for me.
   Holy his name!

Angelus

Er kann morgens, mittags und abends gebetet werden, um uns zu erinnern, dass Gott Sohn zu unserem Heil Mensch geworden ist.

V: Der Engel des Herrn brachte Maria die Botschaft

A: und sie empfing vom Heiligen Geist.

Gegrüßet seist du, Maria...

V: Maria sprach: Siehe, ich bin die Magd des Herrn

A: mir geschehe nach Deinem Wort.

Gegrüßet seist du, Maria...

V: Und das Wort ist Fleisch geworden

A: und hat unter uns gewohnt.

Gegrüßet seist du, Maria...

V: Bitte für uns heilige Gottesmutter

A: auf dass wir würdig werden der Verheißungen Christi.

Lasset uns beten: Allmächtiger Gott, gieße deine Gnade in unsere Herzen ein. Durch die Botschaft des Engels haben wir die Menschwerdung Christi, deines Sohnes, erkannt. Lass uns durch sein Leiden und Kreuz ✠ zur Herrlichkeit der Auferstehung gelangen. Darum bitten wir durch Christus, unseren Herrn. **A: Amen.**

Magnificat

Meine Seele preist die Größe des Herrn,
und mein Geist jubelt über Gott, meinen Retter.
Denn auf die Niedrigkeit seiner Magd hat er geschaut.
Siehe, von nun an preisen mich selig alle Geschlechter.
Denn der Mächtige hat Großes an mir getan,
und sein Name ist heilig.

His mercy is from age to age,
on those who fear him.
He puts forth his arm in strength
and scatters the proud-hearted.
He casts the mighty from their thrones
and raises the lowly.
He fills the starving with good things,
sends the rich away empty.
He protects Israel, his servant,
remembering his mercy,
the mercy promised to our fathers,
to Abraham and his sons for ever. (*Lk* 1:46-55)
Glory be to the Father ...

THE HOLY ROSARY

I. The Five Joyful Mysteries (Mondays, Saturdays)

1. The Annunciation.
2. The Visitation.
3. The Nativity.
4. The Presentation in the Temple.
5. The Finding of the Child Jesus in the Temple.

II. The Five Mysteries of Light (Thursdays)

1. The Baptism of the Lord.
2. The Marriage at Cana.
3. The Proclamation of the Kingdom.
4. The Transfiguration.
5. The Institution of the Eucharist.

Er erbarmt sich von Geschlecht zu Geschlecht
über alle, die ihn fürchten.
Er vollbringt mit seinem Arm machtvolle Taten:
Er zerstreut, die im Herzen voll Hochmut sind.
Er stürzt die Mächtigen vom Thron
und erhöht die Niedrigen.
Die Hungernden beschenkt er mit seinen Gaben
und lässt die Reichen leer ausgehen.
Er nimmt sich seines Knechtes Israel an
und denkt an sein Erbarmen,
das er unseren Vätern verheißen hat,
Abraham und seinen Nachkommen auf ewig.
(*Lukas* 1,46-55) Ehre sei dem Vater ...

DER ROSENKRANZ

I. Die freudenreichen Geheimnisse (montags, samstags):

1. Jesus, den du, o Jungfrau, vom Heiligen Geist
   empfangen hast.
2. Jesus, den du, o Jungfrau, zu Elisabeth getragen hast.
3. Jesus, den du, o Jungfrau, (in Betlehem) geboren hast.
4. Jesus, den du, o Jungfrau, im Tempel aufgeopfert hast.
5. Jesus, den du, o Jungfrau, im Tempel wiedergefunden hast.

II. Die lichtreichen Geheimnisse (donnerstags):

1. Jesus, der von Johannes getauft worden ist.
2. Jesus, der sich bei der Hochzeit in Kana offenbart hat.
3. Jesus, der uns das Reich Gottes vekündet hat.
4. Jesus, der auf dem Berg verklärt worden ist.
5. Jesus, der uns die Eucharistie geschenkt hat.

III. The Five Sorrowful Mysteries (Tuesdays, Fridays)

1. The Prayer and Agony in the Garden.
2. The Scourging at the Pillar.
3. The Crowning with Thorns.
4. The Carrying of the Cross.
5. The Crucifixion and Death of our Lord.

IV. The Five Glorious Mysteries (Wednesdays, Sundays)

1. The Resurrection.
2. The Ascension of Christ into Heaven.
3. The Descent of the Holy Spirit on the Apostles.
4. The Assumption.
5. The Coronation of the Blessed Virgin Mary in Heaven and the Glory of all the Saints.

The Hail Holy Queen

Hail, holy Queen, mother of mercy; hail, our life, our sweetness, and our hope! To you do we cry, poor banished children of Eve; to you do we send up our sighs, mourning and weeping in this vale of tears. Turn then, most gracious advocate, your eyes of mercy towards us; and after this our exile, show to us the blessed fruit of your womb, Jesus. O clement, O loving, O sweet Virgin Mary.

V. Pray for us, O holy Mother of God.

R. That we may be made worthy of the promises of Christ.

Let us pray:

O God, whose only-begotten Son, by his life, death and resurrection, has purchased for us the rewards of eternal

III. Die schmerzhaften Geheimnisse (dienstags, freitags):

1. Jesus, der für uns Blut geschwitzt hat.
2. Jesus, der für uns gegeißelt worden ist.
3. Jesus, der für uns mit Dornen gekrönt worden ist.
4. Jesus, der für uns das schwere Kreuz getragen hat.
5. Jesus, der für uns gekreuzigt worden ist.

IV. Die glorreichen Geheimnisse (mittwochs, sonntags):

1. Jesus, der von den Toten auferstanden ist.
2. Jesus, der in den Himmel aufgefahren ist.
3. Jesus, der uns den Heiligen Geist gesandt hat
4. Jesus, der dich, o Jungfrau, in den Himmel
   aufgenommen hat.
5. Jesus, der dich, o Jungfrau, im Himmel gekrönt hat.

Sei gegrüßt, o Königin

Sei gegrüßt, o Königin, Mutter der Barmherzigkeit, unser Leben, unsere Wonne und unsere Hoffnung sei gegrüßt! Zu dir rufen wir, verbannte Kinder Evas; zu dir seufzen wir trauernd und weinend in diesem Tal der Tränen. Wohl an denn, unsere Fürsprecherin, wende deine barmherzigen Augen uns zu, und nach diesem Elend zeige uns Jesus, die gebenedeite Frucht deines Leibes, o gütige, o milde, o süße Jungfrau Maria.

V: Bitte für uns, o heilige Gottesmutter.

R: Auf dass wir würdig werden der Verheißungen Christi.

Lasset uns beten: **V:** O Gott, dein eingeborener Sohn hat uns durch sein Leben, seinen Tod und seine Auferstehung die Schätze des ewigen Lebens erworben. Gewähre uns, wir beschwören dich, dass wir, indem

life; grant, we beseech you, that meditating on these Mysteries of the most holy Rosary of the Blessed Virgin Mary, we may both imitate what they contain, and obtain what they promise, through the same Christ our Lord.
R. Amen.

LITANY OF THE BLESSED VIRGIN MARY

Lord have mercy.
Lord have mercy.
Christ have mercy.
Christ have mercy.
Lord have mercy.
Lord have mercy.
Christ hear us.
Christ graciously hear us.
God the Father of heaven,
have mercy on us. (repeat)
God the Son, Redeemer of the world,
God the Holy Spirit,
Holy Trinity, one God,
Holy Mary,
pray for us. (repeat)
Holy Mother of God,
Holy Virgin of virgins,
Mother of Christ,
Mother of divine grace,
Mother most pure,
Mother most chaste,
Mother inviolate,
Mother undefiled,
Mother most lovable,
Mother most admirable,
Mother of good counsel,
Mother of our Creator,
Mother of our Saviour,
Virgin most prudent,
Virgin most venerable,
Virgin most renowned,
Virgin most powerful,
Virgin most merciful,
Virgin most faithful,
Mirror of justice,
Seat of wisdom,
Cause of our joy,
Spiritual vessel,
Vessel of honour,
Singular vessel of devotion,
Mystical rose,

wir diese Geheimnisse im überaus heiligen Rosenkranz der gebenedeiten Jungfrau Maria betrachten, dazu fähig werden, nachzuahmen, was sie enthalten, und zu erlangen, was sie verheißen, durch denselben Christus, unseren Herrn. **A: Amen.**

LAURETANISCHE LITANEI

Herr, erbarme Dich
Herr, erbarme Dich
Christus, erbarme Dich
Christus, erbarme Dich
Herr, erbarme Dich
Herr, erbarme Dich
Christus höre uns
Christus erhöre uns
Gott Vater im Himmel,
erbarme Dich unser (dieser
Ruf wird wiederholt)
Gott Sohn, Erlöser der Welt
Gott Heiliger Geist
Heiligste dreifaltiger Gott
Heilige Maria
bitte für uns. (dieser Ruf
wird wiederholt)
Heilige Mutter Gottes
Heilige Jungfrau über
allen Jungfrauen
Mutter Christi
Mutter der Kirche

Mutter der göttlichen Gnade
Du reine Mutter
Du keusche Mutter
Du unversehrte Mutter
Du unbefleckte Mutter
Du liebenswürdige Mutter
Du wunderbare Mutter
Du Mutter des guten Rates
Du Mutter des Schöpfers
Du Mutter des Erlösers
Du kluge Jungfrau
Du ehrwürdige Jungfrau
Du lobwürdige Jungfrau
Du mächtige Jungfrau
Du gütige Jungfrau
Du getreue Jungfrau
Du Spiegel der Gerechtigkeit
Du Thron der Weisheit
Du Ursache unserer Freude
Du Kelch des Geistes
Du kostbarer Kelch
Du Kelch der Hingabe

Tower of David,
Tower of ivory,
House of gold,
Ark of the covenant,
Gate of heaven,
Morning Star,
Health of the sick,
Refuge of sinners,
Comfort of the afflicted,
Help of Christians,
Queen of Angels,
Queen of Patriarchs,
Queen of Prophets,
Queen of Apostles
Queen of Martyrs,
Queen of Confessors,
Queen of Virgins,
Queen of all Saints,
Queen conceived
without original sin,
Queen assumed into heaven,
Queen of the most
holy Rosary,
Queen of the Family,
Queen of Peace.

Lamb of God, you take away the sins of the world,
Spare us, O Lord
Lamb of God, you take away the sins of the world,
Graciously hear us, O Lord
Lamb of God, you take away the sins of the world,
Have mercy on us
V. Pray for us, O holy Mother of God.
R. That we may be made worthy of the promises of Christ.
V. *Let us pray:* Lord God, give to your people the joy of
continual health in mind and body. With the prayers of the
Virgin Mary to help us, guide us through the sorrows of this
life to eternal happiness in the life to come. Grant this through
our Lord Jesus Christ, your Son, who lives and reigns with
you and the Holy Spirit, one God, for ever and ever.
R. Amen.

Du geheimnisvolle Rose
Du starker Turm Davids
Du elfenbeinerner Turm
Du goldenes Haus
Du Bundeslade
Du Pforte des Himmels
Du Morgenstern
Du Heil der Kranken
Du Zuflucht der Sünder
Du Trösterin der Betrübten
Du Helferin der Christen
Du Königin der Engel
Du Königin der Patriarchen
Du Königin der Propheten
Du Königin der Apostel
Du Königin der Märtyrer
Du Königin der Bekenner
Du Königin der Jungfrauen
Du Königin aller Heiligen
Du Königin, ohne
Erbsünde empfangen
Du Königin, aufgenommen
in den Himmel
Du Königin vom heiligen
Rosenkranz
Du Königin des Friedens

Lamm Gottes, Du nimmst hinweg die Sünden der Welt,
verschone uns, o Herr.
Lamm Gottes, Du nimmst hinweg die Sünden der Welt,
erhöre uns, o Herr.
Lamm Gottes, Du nimmst hinweg die Sünden der Welt,
erbarme Dich unser.
V: Bitte für uns, heilige Gottesmutter,
A: auf dass wir würdig werden der Verheißungen Christi.
V: *Lasset uns beten:* Gütiger Gott, du hast allen
Menschen Maria zur Mutter gegeben; höre auf ihre
Fürsprache; nimm von uns die Traurigkeit dieser Zeit,
dereinst aber gib uns die ewige Freude. Durch Christus,
unsern Herrn.
A: Amen.

The Memorare

Remember, O most loving Virgin Mary, that it is a thing unheard of, that anyone ever had recourse to your protection, implored your help, or sought your intercession, and was left forsaken. Filled therefore with confidence in your goodness I fly to you, O Mother, Virgin of virgins. To you I come, before you I stand, a sorrowful sinner. Despise not my poor words, O Mother of the Word of God, but graciously hear and grant my prayer. Amen.

The Regina Cæli

V. O Queen of heaven, rejoice! Alleluia.

R. For he whom you did merit to bear. Alleluia.

V. Has risen as he said. Alleluia.

R. Pray for us to God. Alleluia.

V. Rejoice and be glad, O Virgin Mary. Alleluia.

R. For the Lord has risen indeed. Alleluia.

Let us pray: God our Father, you give joy to the world by the resurrection of your Son, our Lord Jesus Christ. Through the prayers of his mother, the Virgin Mary, bring us to the happiness of eternal life. We ask this through our Lord Jesus Christ, your Son, who lives and reigns with you and the Holy Spirit, one God, for ever and ever. **R. Amen.**

Das Memorare

Gedenke, o gütigste Jungfrau Maria, es ist noch nie gehört worden, dass jemand, der zu dir seine Zuflucht nahm, deinen Beistand anrief und um deine Fürbitte flehte, von dir verlassen worden ist. Von diesem Vertrauen beseelt, nehme ich meine Zuflucht zu dir, o Jungfrau der Jungfrauen, meine Mutter, zu dir komme ich, vor dir stehe ich als ein sündiger Mensch. O Mutter des ewigen Wortes, verschmähe nicht meine Worte, sondern höre sie gnädig an und erhöre mich. Amen

Regina Caeli

V: Freu dich, du Himmelskönigin, Halleluja!

A: Den du zu tragen würdig warst, Halleluja.

V: er ist auferstanden, wie er gesagt hat, Halleluja.

A: Bitt Gott für uns, Halleluja.

V: Freu dich und frohlocke, Jungfrau Maria, Halleluja,

A: denn der Herr ist wahrhaft auferstanden, Halleluja.

Lasset uns beten: Allmächtiger Gott, durch die Auferstehung deines Sohnes, unseres Herrn Jesus Christus, hast du die Welt mit Jubel erfüllt. Lass uns durch seine jungfräuliche Mutter Maria zur unvergänglichen Osterfreude gelangen. Darum bitten wir durch Christus, unsern Herrn. **A: Amen.**

An Act of Contrition

O my God, I am sorry and beg pardon for all my sins, and detest them above all things, because they deserve your dreadful punishments, because they have crucified my loving Saviour Jesus Christ, and, most of all, because they offend your infinite goodness; and I firmly resolve, by the help of your grace, never to offend you again, and carefully to avoid the occasions of sin. Amen.

Act of Faith

My God, I believe in you and all that your Church teaches, because you have said it, and your word is true.

Act of Hope

My God, I hope in you, for grace and for glory, because of your promises, your mercy and your power.

Act of Charity

My God, because you are so good, I love you with all my heart, and for your sake, I love my neighbour as myself.

Akt der Reue

O mein Gott, alle meine Sünden sind mir von ganzem Herzen leid, weil ich dich erzürnt und dafür Strafe verdient habe, besonders aber sind sie mir leid, weil ich dich, meinen besten Vater und größten Wohltäter, das höchste und liebenswürdigste Gut beleidigt habe. Ich nehme mir ernstlich vor, nicht mehr zu sündigen und mich wahrhaft zu bessern. O Gott, hilf mir dazu mit deiner Gnade! Amen.

Akt des Glaubens

Mein Gott, ich glaube an Dich und das, was die katholische Kirche lehrt, weil du es gesagt hast und dein Wort wahr ist. Amen.

Akt der Hoffnung

Herr und Gott, ich hoffe, dass ich durch deine Gnade die Vergebung aller Sünden und nach diesem Leben die ewige Seligkeit erlange. Denn du hast das versprochen, der du unendlich mächtig, treu, gütig und barmherzig bist. In dieser Hoffnung will ich leben und sterben. Amen.

Akt der Nächstenliebe

Mein Gott, ich liebe dich von ganzem Herzen, vor allen Dingen weil du unendlich gut und liebenswürdig bist; Durch deine Liebe will ich auch meinen Nächsten lieben wie mich selbst und ihm seine Schuld vergeben. Herr, ich will dich immer mehr lieben. Amen.

Eternal Rest

V. Eternal rest grant to them, O Lord.

R. And let perpetual light shine upon them.

V. May they rest in peace.

R. Amen.

V. O Lord, hear my prayer.

R. And let my cry come to you.

Let us pray:

O God, the Creator and Redeemer of all the faithful, grant to the souls of your servants departed the remission of all their sins, that through our pious supplication they may obtain that pardon which they have always desired; who live and reign for ever and ever. **R. Amen.**

Prayer to my Guardian Angel

O angel of God, my guardian dear to whom God's love commits me here. Ever this night (day) be at my side to light, to guard, to rule and guide. Amen.

Anima Christi

Soul of Christ, sanctify me.

Body of Christ, save me.

Blood of Christ, inebriate me.

Water from the side of Christ, wash me.

Passion of Christ, strengthen me.

O good Jesus, hear me.

Ewige Ruhe

V: Herr, gib ihm/ihr die ewige Ruhe.

A: Und das ewige Licht leuchte ihnen.

V: Herr, lass sie ruhen in Frieden.

A: Amen.

V: Herr, erhöre mein Gebet.

A: Und lass mein Rufen zu dir kommen.

Lasset uns beten:

Gott, du Schöpfer und Erlöser aller Gläubigen, gewähre den Seelen deiner Diener (und Dienerinnen) Nachlaß aller Sünden; so laß sie allzeit ersehnte Verzeihung durch fromme Fürbitte erlangen. Der du lebst und regierst von Ewigkeit zu Ewigkeit. **A: Amen.**

Gebet zu meinem Schutzengel

Engel Gottes, mein Beschützer,
Gott hat dich gesandt, mich zu begleiten.
Erleuchte, beschütze,
leite und führe mich. Amen.

Seele Christi, heilige mich

Seele Christi, heilige mich,
Leib Christi, rette mich,
Blut Christi, tränke mich,
Wasser der Seite Christi, reinige mich,
Leiden Christi, stärke mich,
O guter Jesus, erhöre mich.

Within thy wounds hide me.
Suffer me not to be separated from thee.
From the malicious enemy defend me.
In the hour of my death call me,
And bid me to come to thee.
That with thy saints I may praise thee,
For all eternity. Amen.

Under your protection

We fly to thy protection, O holy Mother of God. Despise not our petitions in our necessities, but deliver us always from all dangers O glorious and blessed Virgin.

Birg in deinen Wunden mich,
von dir lass nimmer scheiden mich,
vor dem bösen Feind beschütze mich.
In meiner Todesstunde rufe mich,
zu dir kommen heiße mich,
mit deinen Heiligen zu loben dich
in deinem Reiche ewiglich. Amen.

Unter Deinen Schutz und Schirm

Unter deinen Schutz und Schirm fliehen wir, o heilige
Gottesgebärerin. Verschmähe nicht unser Gebet in
unseren Nöten, sondern erlöse uns jederzeit von allen
Gefahren, o du glorreiche und gebenedeite Jungfrau,
unsere Frau, unsere Mittlerin, unsere Fürsprecherin.
Versöhne uns mit deinem Sohne, empfiehl uns deinem
Sohne, stelle uns vor deinem Sohne.